A Palace of Waning

A collection of poems by

Pamela Nocerino

Finishing Line Press
Georgetown, Kentucky

A Palace of Waning

For Mark

ACKNOWLEDGMENTS

The following poems were originally published in:

Gyroscope Review: Mercury
Renaissance Review: Bird Slam
Jerry Jazz Musician: Beyond Scale
Welter, Univ of Baltimore: Icy in Sports
Writing in a Woman's Voice: The Tight Possible, Some
boats against the current: Hush
Red Skies: Without Holiday
Gyroscope Review: Posterior Cortical Atrophy
boats against the current: Clam Diggers

Publisher: Leah Huete de Maines
Editor: Christen Kincaid
Cover Art: Pamela Nocerino
Author Photo: Pamela Nocerino
Cover Design: Elizabeth Maines McCleavy

Order online: www.finishinglinepress.com
         also available on amazon.com

Author inquiries and mail orders:
Finishing Line Press
PO Box 1626
Georgetown, Kentucky 40324
USA

Contents

HOME

Mercury

I move through my neighborhood
and lean into sound as transport—
a torn fabric flaps
like fall aspens quaking,
a truck beeps in reverse
like a crow's warning caw

I unmake the concrete
and imagine a path between
trees not planted like soldiers

and I'm brought home
to riverside shade,
on boulders not big enough
to stop the flood
that changed
everything

Remember
how I brought you there
as witness
with skin as testament
in cradles of pine
and I believed in forever
for the last time

I turned then,
as I do now,
from wind and rain
with their warnings
of what I have yet to accept
about seasons

Breckenridge

When snow beckons,
smooth between pines,
in solid waves of invitation

I wander off trail
and wager each step,
breathing ragged gasps
against Winter's solace.

I sink
float
and shiver with the buried.

My footprints cleave a promise
of a way back,
but it's the sound
of spring,
barely crackling beneath,
that brings me home.

Returning

One bird
silent
with poppy-red plumes,
no bigger than
my clenched hand,
stays
as I go by.

My attention puffs
her inattention
and confident nearness.
She knows I'm leaving.
Her quiet is the gift
I am to take.

Her thread-thin legs
are grounded like trunks
in spite of
the waiting sky.
She has something
to say that Earth needs to hear
and I am to bear witness.
Her black wings remain stoic
against the begging wind.
And then she shivers

and stills

until I acknowledge
that I have flown too.

Bird Slam

Our windows
are not that clean
but the birds hurt themselves
anyway

and I startle
from a page of prose or verse
like we crashed into each other
in separate skies

and both fell,
but not to the ground.

I stare up and through,
blank,
until I find words again.

They are on the floor,
which page?
Ah yes, the perfect pairing
of butterscotch with light.

Yes,
  there,
    lift.

Beyond Scale

Our love is a jazz trio
in last-set energy
with expanded structures
and smoky-toned fusion.

Wandering in melodies
of our own inner worlds,
we hold pauses like brinks
just long enough for longing.

We roil the melody
with solos rising and spilling
toward each other without caution
in scattered wholeness.

Even the bridge's
wild independence
is at the mercy of progression.
It tangles back and reminds us
we are home.

Scatter

Like a cutting,   g
    you root   n
                             i

    separate and reach

Aren't you sad?
I'm asked
as you find
your own light

There are many leavings,
I answer.

    Distance is but one.

We are only seeds
—scattered and thirsty—
resting awhile
in fertile beginnings

until

we're split wide open
                  again

ICY IN SPOTS

Red neon blinks
like it celebrates the danger,
and we take it, as tradition dictates,
as a triple dare
to trundle out
with calendars as stuffed as our bellies.

The car warms
and one of us begins the annual tale
of sliding tires
in a spinning car
before seatbelts
when I70 was only two lanes
and Grandma folded her body around
the tin of her powdered pecan cookies.

"Nothing was broken!"
we all yell together,
referring to bones and cookies
but not in that order.
The person holding this year's batch
feels the weight of their responsibility,
and repositions the old tin
for the fifth time on their lap
as the car pulls out.

The details slip with each retelling.
It's not always Grandma who protects the cookies,
but it is always those cookies.
And the ending still keeps us on the road—

Nothing is broken.

SELF

The Tight Possible

If I felt worthy
of the love
I offer others,
what would
tick, spin,
loosen, or cling?
The long songs
of Sundays
and midnights
would hum
in what key?
I drum
evergreen needles
like jazz brushes
against the tight
possible
and try.

The Hard Work

When I
try to look
directly into
Self,
it scampers
to periphery
like Puck
squeezing his
perceiving potion.

It's only
when I drop
my guard
and focus
on a tiny linger
or a thick pause,
that insight
slams into me.

It's only then
that the Self
is exposed.
I grab the sprite,
and twist it,
wring it for
the vulnerable
unwringing
in the fresh
outside—
petals and
all.

Hush

The hush
hush
hush
of rhythmic waves
uncover and bury
the shells of the lives I imagined
& the life I carry—
the space between as vast and blurry
as the crepuscular horizon.
Wet lines of tide mark
what was and what will be again.
My faltering steps,
a moment at best,
fill with sea and retreat
as I embrace the light dullness
of essential insignificance.

Some

Women are back
to nothing again today
in a country far from me—
their personhood revoked
like a license
because some turned away

And I am here
impaired by freedoms
claimed by some
in proud lairs of personhood
where gender
is but one offense

We are all
falling backward
in the fight for
the right
to turn
some
away

Beauty Fatigue

I speak you
as my first language
in repetitive prose of touch
and shuddering carnage
of muscle & crevice
Familiar landscapes of neck and taste
loosen me in garlands of shadow—
baiting and abating
pause.
I press against your scent
to slumber in—
and surrender to—
the delicate poverties
your beauty imposes.

Without Holiday

The steam of too hot tea
on another eve of absence
blurs my view of holiday lights
in the window.

We shouldn't ask a memory
too much, I know,
but I do know the gift of you
unmasked and near.

I reopen you each day
in this distance
and your light, as certain as sun,
is bright and clear.

Our past laughter layers
like harmonies
in this wrapping and unraveling
of quarantine.

I wander in our memories,
asking them too much,
but you surprise me with great comfort
every time.

LOSS

Posterior Cortical Atrophy

The first taste of losing you
was hot springs sulfur on our swimsuits
I held your shoulders hard
You tried to breathe in your panic
Our eyes met briefly
and I couldn't
find you
tie you
to anxiety/menopause/stress—
so many ways to dismiss
a fall at work
a car crashing
by itself
crumpled by
the police officer
condescending
descending
losing the flavor of you
lose the car/the job/the house
move into
Mama's fresh grief—
and I come weekly
to your side
inside
one room looping news
consumes and ruins
your hunger for all
that you were
that we were
together

Hawk Migration

There were so many
then none
and I wept

But I should've known
about death
and return
but I didn't

Their beauty
and fierce violence
overwhelmed me
as I stared

watching them
savage and
pose in regal profiles
confident
on my posts

I envied their
thick-knickered thighs
and feathered jackets

There were so many
then none
not one

I should've
known
but I didn't

Queer

I edited the word out
of a poem in my classroom
when it meant 'strange' in context
because I was afraid to discuss
all of the other glorious meanings
with 11-year-olds
and their angry parents.

I asked you if that was okay,
as if your permission absolved me.
You were gracious, as always,
but I was wrong,
and should've apologized then.

I'm sorry.

Isn't it amazing how afraid
of power
we can be,
when that's exactly how
we give it away.

Tremor

Your gift to me is
no hope of solid ground,
an intermittent intimacy
of circumstance
that offers no haven
and forces my refuge inward—
six feet need-deep—
where I discover
new ways to surface
far from fault lines.

Distance

In your solid love,
away from worlds
of screens and
fearful imagination,
I am three-dimensional
in my place
within our story.
But distance—

both real
and near in your welded unspoken—

melts me
like waiting ice
and changes form
enough
to make unrecognizable
the design
before
the separation.

Buoy

Thank you for coming to me
in your dark hair without chemo curls,
to dip your laughing face in and out of a smooth ocean surface—
smooth because we're out so far past the breaks
of this world's pain and illness.

You always loved the water.
Remember when you wrapped your middle
in clinging plastic and jumped
into the ocean
when you shouldn't
and you lived,
and live now
in that last visit of pure joy
before
you left this earth.

And now I try to wrap my grief
in plastic and jump in with you,
but I continually resurface unbound.

Filing

It's like stepping on sponges—
the breaking of things.

Sign here.

Flattening until
the memory of fullness
feels like a lie.

And here.

Shoving everything out
until dry
and walking away.

And finally,
There.

PLACE

Rise

The sun doesn't rise
We rotate to see it,
neither by choice
nor despair,
neither desire
nor apathy.
Its predictable warmth
is forced upon us
by tilt
and more,
whether we are willing
to cherish it
or hide away.
But we prefer verbs
of hope,
like rise,
rather than
the solid,
hot movement
of Truth.

Clam Diggers

Hidden muscles fold and bend
like accordions
to dig in mourning sand.
Dawn reveals stretched, wide belly creases
in briefly upright shore hunters
who decide what to keep and
what to release—
a bewitching sort
to witness—
alike, in its way,
to memories
locked tight and left buried
without heat
to open and consume,
like mussels,
for tomorrow's bending.

Art emergency!

Something halts you
with its beauty—
a painting, a poem, a film—
and you text me to share
that sacred overwhelm.
I am rescued equally
by the art

and your inclusion.

Emily Says

You are not
a Nobody too!
In fact—you're famous
And worshipped in a way
That makes me pavonine
Whenever I Name-drop—
Casually of course—
That we're friends
You and me!
In this bog of life—
This marsh of messy
This grit and grace
With too much alliteration
And pompous references—
Where most importantly—

There's a pair of us.

Corsets

Stays from a dead whale
strained against nature
to pronounce false cores.

Out of view, out of the way,
lungs, organs, and flesh retreated
and silenced deep songs.

Fragile, bound shapes called
like helpless sirens
and trapped want in hourglasses.

Oh, but when we rested, we knew.
No strain of lace or steel or wood
could cinch the girth of our knowing.

To breathe fully is to fight back.

The sands of time broke open
and shifted shapes
into Mother Hubbard freedoms.

Victorian news responded to the waste—
"A vandalism of beauty!"
"An inconvenience of pleasure!"

But the same women
who helped each other fasten,
help each other
unfasten

and like baleen,
we sieve
gaze and expectation
for what we want
to swallow.

Big History

Old dead,
newly uncovered,
reposition the
understanding
of our place
with-in it all.
Old revolutions,
newly discovered,
remap our
understanding
of our place
with-out it all.
Still.
The gravity
of Self
burns fixed and fused
to the core
of need—
here
and now.

Revolution

The expanding world spins
and spirals
and spits
and swallows
to meet itself
again
and again
repetitive only to those
who make lines
to define
an ending that was
never never
there.

Pamela Nocerino is a writer who once helped build a giant troll in the Rocky Mountains. She enjoyed a brief career on stage in Denver until she needed health insurance and became a dedicated middle school teacher for over 20 years. Pamela earned a BA in Theatre Arts and an MA in Communication. Although she's been writing since she was 10, she started submitting work during the pandemic lockdown and now has published poetry, fiction, nonfiction, short plays, songs, and essays. Born in Illinois, she's a Colorado transplant dedicating her third act to creative exploration and mindful connection. When not working, she's reading and... sometimes she hikes, goes to plays, blares music, and cooks with friends, but mostly she's reading. Pamela has received awards for acting, teaching, and songwriting, but that troll time in Breckenridge remains a highlight.

WEBSITE   https://www.pamelanocerino.com/

www.ingramcontent.com/pod-product-compliance
Lightning Source LLC
Chambersburg PA
CBHW022050080426
42734CB00009B/1289